Animal Adaptations

Metamorphosis

JACK ZAYARNY

www.av2books.com

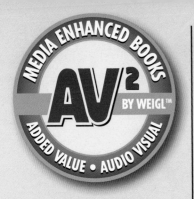

Go to www.av2books.com, and enter this book's unique code.

BOOK CODE

B 7 7 6 7 7 4

AV² by Weigl brings you media enhanced books that support active learning.

AV² provides enriched content that supplements and complements this book. Weigl's AV² books strive to create inspired learning and engage young minds in a total learning experience.

Your AV² Media Enhanced books come alive with...

Audio
Listen to sections of the book read aloud.

Key Words
Study vocabulary, and complete a matching word activity.

Video
Watch informative video clips.

Quizzes
Test your knowledge.

Embedded Weblinks
Gain additional information for research.

Slide Show
View images and captions, and prepare a presentation.

Try This!
Complete activities and hands-on experiments.

... and much, much more!

Published by AV² by Weigl
350 5th Avenue, 59th Floor
New York, NY 10118
Websites: www.av2books.com   www.weigl.com

Library of Congress Control Number: 2014941762

ISBN 978-1-4896-1374-5 (hardcover)
ISBN 978-1-4896-1375-2 (softcover)
ISBN 978-1-4896-1376-9 (single-user eBook)
ISBN 978-1-4896-1377-6 (multi-user eBook)

Printed in the United States of America in North Mankato, Minnesota
1 2 3 4 5 6 7 8 9 18 17 16 15 14

062014
WEP090514

Project Coordinator Aaron Carr
Art Director Terry Paulhus

Contents

What Is an Adaptation?

Many animals have **features** that help them survive in their **habitat**. Stronger animals that are better suited to their habitat have more chances to survive than weaker animals. **Natural selection** is a process by which the features of these surviving animals are passed on to their offspring. These features are known as adaptations. Adaptations develop over thousands of years. Fast movement, color, and the ability to survive in heat or cold are some adaptations that help animals survive changing conditions.

Metamorphosis is a special type of adaptation. It allows an animal to survive in more than one habitat. A frog starts life as an egg, then it hatches into a tadpole. Tadpoles live in the water and eat small insects. After changing, or metamorphosizing, into an adult form, frogs spend more of their lives on land. This change in habitat allows the **species** to be more flexible.

Frogs eat larger flying insects, such as mosquitoes and dragonflies.

5

AMAZING ADAPTATIONS

Some animals change body shapes, or metamorphose, in interesting ways.

Tiger Salamander

Salamanders hatch from eggs and begin life as tiny copies of the adults. However, they have a shorter body, and **gills** and fins on the outside. Both of these are taken back into the body when they change into an adult.

House Fly

Flies begin their lives as eggs, which hatch into worm-like maggots. Each maggot then turns into a pupa. Inside the pupa, the maggot remakes itself into an adult fly.

Monarch Butterfly

The Monarch butterfly metamorphoses from an egg to a caterpillar, then into a **chrysalis**, and on to a butterfly.

Ladybug

Ladybugs lay their eggs near aphids. When the **larvae** hatch, they will each eat up to 25 aphids a day. Larvae will shed their skin, or molt, several times before becoming a pupa, and then an adult ladybug.

Mantis Shrimp

The larvae of the mantis shrimp looks very different to the adult. As they grow, mantis shrimp shed, or molt, their hard outer covering. It takes several weeks for the new covering to harden.

What Is Metamorphosis?

Most insects, some **amphibians**, and some **crustaceans** go through big changes during their life cycle. These changes are known as metamorphosis. Metamorphosis may cause the animal to change its physical characteristics and behavior. The adaptation of metamorphosis allows the animal to survive, produce offspring, and spread around its habitat.

LARVAE STAGE

Larvae hatch from eggs and often look completely different than the adults. The larvae feed constantly. This feeding provides the energy for the next big change.

PUPA STAGE

During the pupa stage, the animal is protected inside a cocoon or chrysalis. The chrysalis does not move, but many exciting changes happen inside. The body of the larva breaks down, and the adult body is formed.

ADULT STAGE

At the end of the pupa stage, the adult butterfly breaks free of the chrysalis. It is now ready to fly and find a mate.

METAMORPHOSIS OF THE GRASSHOPPER

The life cycle of a grasshopper has three stages.
These stages are egg, nymph, and adult. Each stage
adds more features to the grasshopper.

Egg Stage

Grasshoppers lay their eggs in soil or leaf litter. After about 10 months, the eggs hatch.

Nymph Stage

After hatching, the young grasshopper is called a nymph. Nymphs are very small, do not have wings, and are mainly built to feed. A nymph needs to molt to increase in size. Each period between molting is known as an instar.

Adult Stage

After a number of instars, the adult grasshopper finishes its development. It has wings and no longer molts. The adult is now ready to find a mate.

What Does It Do?

Metamorphosis can play an important role within a **food web**. Often, larvae begin life near a supply of food. Monarch butterflies and other insects lay their eggs on plants that their larvae will eat. Other animals, such as frogs, hatch their young at a time of year that best suits the needs of their offspring.

Larvae often eat different food than adults of the same species. This means that the larvae and the adults are not competing for food. This makes the animal more likely to survive at each stage of development. The ability to move from one habitat, such as water, to another habitat, such as land, at different stages of development also helps a species to survive.

Butterflies often lay their eggs on the leaves of milkweed plants. As soon as they hatch, the caterpillars will start to eat the leaves.

Garden Food Web

In a garden food web, aphids feed on plants such as roses. Ladybugs lay their eggs near aphid **colonies**. As the eggs hatch into ladybug larvae, the larvae have a plentiful supply of aphids to eat. Adult ladybugs are eaten by small birds such as robins. These small birds are, in turn, hunted by larger **predatory** birds such as hawks.

Plant

Hawk

Aphid

Robin

Ladybug

Types of Metamorphosis

Metamorphosis plays a role in the life cycle of insects, amphibians, and crustaceans. The type of metamorphosis is different for each group. There are two types used by insects. These are complete and incomplete metamorphosis. With complete metamorphosis, the insect looks different at each stage. Insect larvae also eat different food than adult insects. With incomplete metamorphosis, the young insect looks like a smaller version of the adult.

Amphibians develop from larvae known as tadpoles. Their bodies are different at each stage of development. They may have gills as a tadpole and lungs as an adult. They may start life as a **herbivore** and end up as a **carnivore**. Crustaceans such as lobsters, crabs, and shrimp molt several times during their metamorphosis. Each time, their bodies become more complex.

Through the molting process, crustaceans change from larvae with soft, fragile bodies to adults with hard, protective shells.

5 COMPLEX CHANGES

Complete Insect Metamorphosis

The Monarch butterfly metamorphoses from an egg to a caterpillar, to a pupa, then to an adult butterfly.

Incomplete Insect Metamorphosis

Grasshoppers, cockroaches, and dragonflies are some of the insects that go through incomplete metamorphosis. They develop through stages of molting and growing.

Aquatic Insect Metamorphosis

Some **aquatic** insects such as mayflies spend months or years as larvae. Only a short time is spent as an adult, when they find a mate and produce offspring.

Amphibian Metamorphosis

Amphibians, such as frogs, go through a complex metamorphosis. At each stage, the animal looks different, eats different food, and plays a different role in its habitat.

Crustacean Metamorphosis

Similar to the incomplete insect metamorphosis, crustaceans start life as an egg before hatching into a small version of the adult animal. They go through a series of molts, gaining physical features over time.

How Does It Work?

An animal that goes through metatmorphosis is adapted to perform a key function at each stage of its development. A caterpillar, for example, is built for eating, and no other function. It has a mouth, **antennae**, and short legs. The caterpillar body is basically a tube to process food. This form of the animal has no need to find a mate, and no need for great mobility.

When the caterpillar reaches a certain size, it will spin a cocoon if it is to become a moth, or form a chrysalis if it is to become a butterfly. This is known as the pupa stage. Inside the chrysalis or cocoon, **cells** that were not used in the caterpillar stage begin growing to form the body of the adult insect. Meanwhile, the caterpillar cells break down into a soup-like liquid which the new cells use to grow. When the pupa breaks open, a brand-new insect will come out.

It takes about 10 to 14 days for a butterfly to develop inside a chrysalis.

4 STAGES OF FROG METAMORPHOSIS

Egg

Hundreds of eggs are laid at once to increase the chances of some surviving. They are covered in a jelly-like substance for protection.

Tadpole

Eggs hatch into into tadpoles, or frog larvae. Tadpoles live in the water and feed on plants.

Froglet

After some time, tadpoles develop into froglets. Froglets grow legs and their tails begin to shrink.

Adult

The adult frog loses its tail. It grows a tongue, which it uses to catch insects. Its body may continue to grow for some time.

Timeline

In the animal world, the process of natural selection ensures the survival of the species. Adaptations such as metamorphosis help certain animals adapt better to a changing environment. These animals survive longer, find mates, and pass on their adaptations to their offspring. An adaptation such as metamorphosis can be gradually developed and passed on for millions of years, because it allows animals that have it to survive.

Like other grasshoppers, the milkweed grasshopper goes through incomplete metamorphosis. It also has adapted bright coloring to warn predators that it is poisonous to eat.

Insect Metamorphosis

540–520 Million Years Ago

Marine **invertebrates** such as crustaceans and worms appear for the first time. **Fossils** show that these creatures were already capable of metamorphosis.

440–420 Million Years Ago

Many insect species appear. At this time, insects have not developed metamorphosis.

400–350 Million Years Ago

Winged insects appear and develop metamorphosis. Both complete and incomplete metamorphosis is present.

Today

Nearly 85 percent of all insect species go through complete metamorphosis in their life cycles. These include ants and beetles. The rest, such as dragonflies and mayflies, go through incomplete metamorphosis.

How Humans Use Metamorphosis

While people do not go through physical metamorphosis in their lives, metamorphosis does exist in human culture. Technology, in particular, is in a constant state of metamorphosis. People developed steam power, which was followed by coal and oil power. Electricity and solar power could be described as later stages of metamorphosis. Each of these technolgies is connected, but different to each other, in the same way as the stages of animal metamorphosis. In a similar way, the introduction of computers brought a **technological revolution**, or metamorphosis, to modern society.

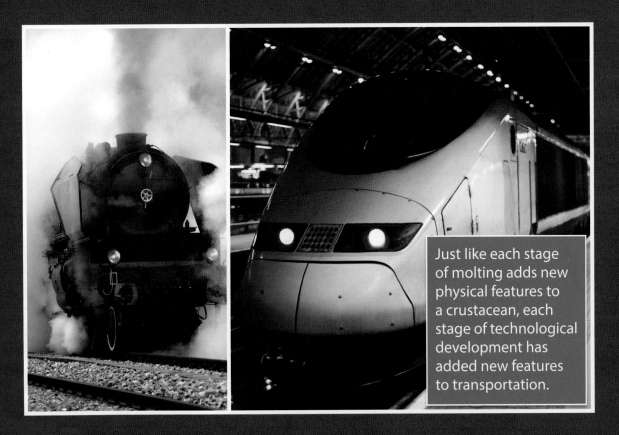

Just like each stage of molting adds new physical features to a crustacean, each stage of technological development has added new features to transportation.

Space flight is an example of people learning from animal metamorphosis. Space shuttles were built with three main parts. These were an external fuel tank, two solid rocket boosters (SRBs), and the shuttle itself. The two SRBs and the external fuel tank were used only to launch the shuttle beyond Earth's **atmosphere**. Once in space, the shuttle transformed, discarding the SRBs and the fuel tank to suit its new environment. This can be compared to a frog discarding the gills of a tadpole once it is transformed into an animal that lives on land.

Once in space, the two SRBs and the external fuel tank were no longer needed.

Metamorphosis and Biodiversity

Biodiversity refers to all the different plants and animals that live in a particular habitat or **biome**. A large variety of different animals and plants allows a biome to function properly. This is because every **organism** has a role to play in the food web. A higher variety of animals also promotes natural selection. The animals with the most effective adaptations survive.

Metamorphosis helps biodiversity, as different stages of development in insects, amphibians, and crustaceans fill various roles in the animals' environments. Mayfly nymphs, for example, are underwater predators that hunt small insects. Mayfly adults provide food for frogs and larger insects such as dragonflies. This variety of habitats and roles within one animal's life cycle supports biodiversity.

Wetlands, marshes, and ponds can be important biomes due to their great biodiversity. These biomes are home to crustaceans, insects, amphibians, fish, birds, mammals, and a variety of plant life.

Tadpoles are underwater animals that eat plants, but they develop into land-based carnivores.

Caterpillars are slow-moving leaf-eating animals that grow into butterflies that feed on the nectar of flowers.

Conservation

Natural environments are finely balanced systems. Upsetting this balance often leads to harm for species living in the habitat. Destruction of trees and natural landscapes can harm living environments for one or more stages of an animal's life cycle. Damaging or changing the environment for even one stage in a species' development can have terrible effects on its ability to survive. If a species dies out or its numbers drop too low, this lack of balance will harm biodiversity and place the survival of many species in danger. To avoid this, many organizations work to protect wildlife environments. Groups such as the International Union for Conservation of Nature (IUCN) and the ranger services for national parks play a key role in the protection of biomes.

By keeping track of the number of different animals in a habitat, scientists help to protect the biodiversity of natural environments.

Activity

Match the animal with the type of metamorphosis that helps it survive.

1 Butterfly

Grasshopper 2

Frog 3

Crab 4

A Crustacean metamorphosis

B Complete amphibian metamorphosis

C Complete insect metamorphosis

D Incomplete insect metamorphosis

Answers: 1. C 2. D 3. B 4. A

Quiz

Complete this quiz to test your knowledge of metamorphosis.

1 What is the next stage in the life cycle of a butterfly after it is a caterpillar?

A. Chrysalis

2 What is the name for periods between molts in insects such as grasshoppers?

A. Instars

3 Which animal do ladybug larvae use as a food source?

A. Aphids

4 Which are the two types of insect metamorphosis?

A. Complete and incomplete

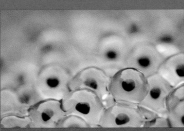

5 What are the four stages of frog metamorphosis?

A. Egg, tadpole, froglet, adult

6 What is the pupa of a moth called?

A. A cocoon

7 How many years ago did insect metamorphosis begin?

A. 400–350 million years ago

8 Which space vehicle is modeled on metamorphosis?

A. Space shuttle

9 What is the name of the larvae of insects such as grasshoppers and mayflies?

A. Nymphs

10 What does a frog grow to help it catch insects?

A. A tongue

Key Words

amphibians: cold-blooded animals that have backbones and moist skin without scales

antennae: a pair of thin, sensitive organs on the head of an insect or crustacean that is used mainly to feel and touch things

aquatic: water

atmosphere: the mixture of gases surrounding Earth

biome: a large community of plants and animals that live in a major habitat, such as a forest

carnivore: an animal that feeds on other animals

cells: the smallest parts, or units, of a living thing

chrysalis: the pupa of a butterfly

colonies: communities of animals and plants

crustaceans: animals that live mostly in water and have hard shells and jointed bodies and legs

features: characteristics of an object or living creature

food web: a system of connected food chains within a habitat

fossils: the remains of ancient plants or animals that have been preserved in rock

gills: the external organs in a fish used for breathing underwater

habitat: the natural environment of a living thing

herbivore: an animal that feeds on plants

invertebrates: animals that do not have backbones

larvae: the immature form of an animal that goes through metamorphosis

metamorphosis: a major change in form or structure of some animals that happens as the animal becomes an adult

natural selection: a natural process where animals that have better adapted to their environment survive and pass on those adaptations to their young

organism: an individual form of life, such as a plant or an animal

predatory: living by killing and eating other animals

species: a group pf plants or animals that are alike in many ways

technological revolution: a period during which new technologies that greatly change people's behavior develop quickly

Index

Log on to www.av2books.com

AV² by Weigl brings you media enhanced books that support active learning. Go to www.av2books.com, and enter the special code found on page 2 of this book. You will gain access to enriched and enhanced content that supplements and complements this book. Content includes video, audio, weblinks, quizzes, a slide show, and activities.

AV² Online Navigation

Book Pages
AV² pages directly correspond to pages in the book.

Audio
Listen to sections of the book read aloud.

Video
Watch informative video clips.

Key Words
Study vocabulary, and complete a matching word activity.

Embedded Weblinks
Gain additional information for research.

Quizzes
Test your knowledge.

Slide Show
View images and captions, and prepare a presentation.

Try This!
Complete activities and hands-on experiments.

AV² was built to bridge the gap between print and digital. We encourage you to tell us what you like and what you want to see in the future.

Sign up to be an AV² Ambassador at www.av2books.com/ambassador.

Due to the dynamic nature of the internet, some of the URLs and activities provided as part of AV² by Weigl may have changed or ceased to exist. AV² by Weigl accepts no responsibility for any such changes. All media enhanced books are regularly monitored to update addresses and sites in a timely manner. Contact AV² by Weigl at 1-866-649-3445 or av2books@weigl.com with any questions, comments, or feedback.